PLANNING YOUR BUSINESS

Forthcoming titles in this series will include

- *Winning Negotiation Tactics*
- *Painless Business Finance*
- *Winning CVs!*
- *Getting Hired!*
- *Managing People for the First Time!*
- *Successful Interviewing Techniques!*
- *Letter Writing for Winners!*
- *Winning Telephone Techniques!*

Do you have any ideas for subjects which could be included in this exciting and innovative series? Could your company benefit from close involvement with a forthcoming title?

Please write to David Grant Publishing Limited
80 Ridgeway, Pembury, Tunbridge Wells, Kent TN2 4EZ
with your ideas or suggestions

PLANNING

YOUR BUSINESS

Richard Burton

60 Minutes Success Skills Series

First published 1998 by
David Grant Publishing Limited
80 Ridgeway
Pembury
Kent TN2 4EZ
United Kingdom

99 98 10 9 8 7 6 5 4 3 2 1

60 Minutes Success Skills Series is an imprint of
David Grant Publishing Limited

British Library Cataloguing in Publication Data
A CIP catalogue record for this book is available from the British Library

ISBN 1-901306-06-2

Cover design: Steve Haynes
Text design: Graham Rich
Production editor: Paul Stringer

Typeset in Futura by
Archetype IT Ltd, web site http://www.archetype-it.com
Printed and bound in Great Britain by
T.J. International Ltd, Padstow, Cornwall

This book is printed on acid-free paper

CONTENTS

Chapter 6: Winning with your business plan   51

Know what your plan is for
Understand what drives the professionals who will read it
Learn how to structure your plan
Develop a strategy for the meeting with your backers

WELCOME

ABOUT *PLANNING YOUR BUSINESS*

This book is part of the 60 Minutes Success Skills Series. Can you *really* learn how to plan to grow your new or recently formed business in just one hour? The answer is a resounding "Yes".

The only bit of waffle in this book

The 60 Minutes Success Skills Series is written for people with neither the time nor the patience to trawl through page after page of jargon, management-speak and space-filling waffle. Many people would have you believe that starting and growing a new business is a dangerous activity that will ruin your health, your marriage and your finances. They say that you've either got to be seriously rich already or very, very lucky to have any chance at all of succeeding. This is nonsense. The financial and personal rewards of starting a business can be colossal, but if there is one critical factor that will determine the fate of your new venture it is the way you *plan* it.

   This book recognises that time is precious. The philosophy of the series is that you can learn all you really need to know quickly and without fuss. The aim is to distil the essential, practical advice so that you can start to use it straight away. Running a growing business will change your life. The hour that you spend with this book will help to ensure that it changes it for the better.

Is this book for you?

Do you ever

   ○ *sit through endless hours at work thinking "this could all be done so much better"?*
   ○ *fantasise on your way home about going it alone?*
   ○ *feel envious as friends and former colleagues talk of the excitement and rewards of running their own shows?*
   ○ *wish that you were able to hand-pick your colleagues instead of having to work with people who constantly let you down?*

If so, you are one of the millions of people worldwide who dream each year of starting their own business. However, you *might* not be suited to it. *Planning Your Business* will help you to evaluate your prospects if you are, and may prevent you making an expensive mistake if you are not.

Why plan anyway? Here are four good reasons:

- ○ *Nobody – especially your financial backers and other professional advisers – will take your business proposals seriously if you don't.*
- ○ *It's the only way to discover how much money you are going to need, and when you are going to need it.*
- ○ *You can make your mistakes in your head (or on paper) – much less painful than making them in the market.*
- ○ *It will force you to look at the future – and the real world your business will be operating in – and not the past, which is largely irrelevant in today's mercurial business climate.*

Don't make the mistake of thinking that planning a business is easy. Research shows that it can take 200 to 400 man hours to plan a business properly. However, in just one hour this book will put you on the right track. It will be time well spent. It will provide the platform for your future.

How to use this book

The message in this book is "it's OK to skim". You don't have to read it all at once, or follow every tip to the letter. *Planning Your Business* has been written to dip into, so feel free to flick through it to find the help you most need. It is a collection of hands-on tips that will help you to plan your business both for the purpose of raising capital and for the long-term health of your venture. In just 60 minutes you can discover exactly what ground you will need to cover to succeed.

You will find that there are graphic features used throughout the book.

This means "something to think about" – it sets the scene and identifies the problems by prompting you to think about situations which should instantly feel familiar.

With the problems diagnosed, these features give you an action plan – this will help you to get your own ideas in order.

This feature appears at the end of each chapter. It is a checklist which condenses all the advice given throughout the chapter. Similar features appear within chapters, all of which are overflowing with practical tips!

As you read through the book you will come across a lot of practical advice. But if you are really pushed for time you can always flick to the tips feature at the end of each chapter to get an instant overview. These are also a useful reminder when you come back to look at this book in the future.

With *Planning Your Business* in your briefcase your new venture is set to fly. Good luck!

Chapter 1

HAVE YOU GOT WHAT IT TAKES?

What's in this chapter for you

> *Know your strengths and weaknesses*
> *Test the big idea*
> *Decide the best structure for your business*
> *Know the likely pitfalls*

> ❝ *One of the best things I ever did for my business was to spend an hour thinking about me – about what I really wanted out of life, and about my **real** skills, not those I had been told I possessed, or that I had built my career on. I had a reputation for being great with people, a true team-builder. In fact I realised that my core characteristic was ruthless determination to win, regardless of others.* ❞
> **– Fern Cawl, telecommunications entrepreneur**

Know your strengths and weaknesses

Growing your business depends on you and no-one else. There is no hiding place for the entrepreneur, and nowhere to shift the blame to. So you need more than just a good idea to go solo. Take a cool look at yourself and what you have achieved. You must be honest – accept that you do have weaknesses but, on the other hand, don't underestimate your strengths.

Ask yourself some searching questions.

❑ *Are you really motivated? Are you self-confident, determined, persistent and realistic? Have you got a positive approach? If you plan to work from home, can you resist the chores you didn't finish at the weekend or the delights of daytime TV?*

❑ *Can you **learn**? Can you accept advice from professional advisers like accountants, solicitors, bankers and so on? Can you also accept setbacks and learn from them? And have you got enough detailed technical knowledge of your business? Do you know when to ask for help?*

❑ *What about your personal circumstances? Have you got the full support of your family? Are you healthy – physically, emotionally and mentally? Be honest – have you got the energy to work harder than ever before, and for longer?*
❑ *Can you sell? Not just your product or service, but yourself too? Do you know the market thoroughly? Are you a good problem solver?*

If the answer to at least 75 per cent of these questions isn't "Yes", you can save 55 minutes of your life by returning this book to the shelf right now. Still here? Great!

This isn't a comprehensive list of the qualities needed to grow a business but it will give you an idea of the sort of profile real entrepreneurs have.

Test the big idea

❝ *I had an idea for a new kind of message service. I loved it so much I was on the verge of investing a lot of capital in it. I was advised to test market it and I discovered to my great shock that most people hated it. It was just too complex and didn't deliver the customer convenience I thought it did. I made my fortune with a completely different service, but that three-day test market saved my business.* ❞
– Fern Cawl

You may think you have an award winning idea for a new product or service, but before you commit everything to it you had better find out! And it's no good just trying it out informally on friends and family. Chances are that they won't have the right background and experience to make a professional judgement, and that they may just tell you what they think you want to hear.

Knowing what your customers want, and what they will want in the future is crucial.
Define your customers carefully. What sort of people are they? Where do they live? How will they want to buy whatever it is you want to supply them with?

Do some 'desk research'. This is largely an information gathering process — getting ideas about the size of your market, trends in it, whether or not it is growing and about your competitors. You can get this information from business reports, government departments and local Chambers of Commerce for instance. A good start will be your local librarian who should be able to point you in the direction of a multitude of sources of very useful statistical information. If you have access to the Internet you may be able to find something useful there too.

Armed with this vital data you can now devise a way to communicate with potential customers to find out more ('field research'). It could be a questionnaire that you mail or a series of visits to interview selected potential customers, a telephone survey or a 'focus group' (test panel). Your business will get off to a very shaky start if you don't have answers to the fundamental questions about your product, your market and your customers.

For instance, what will your offering replace? It could be a competitor's product or service, but it might not be. Even in situations where there is 'no competition' (very rarely the case) remember that if your customer chooses to spend money with you they are also choosing *not* to spend it with someone else. Even if the two products or services seem entirely unconnected remember that you have to think like your customer. Marketing textbooks go on interminably about this — it's about defining what market you are *really* in. It's mostly common sense.

The key to all this is your customer. Don't get preoccupied by the product or service you are planning. *Do* be obsessed by the experience your customers will have of it. *Become* your customer for a while. You must know what difference the existence of your new offering will make to their lives. It could simply be a cheaper version of whatever it is they are experiencing from your competitors. But it could be something much more sophisticated than that. You need to find out. Remember — there's no marketing department to blame now if you get it wrong!

Decide the best structure for your business

❝ *When we set up our fruit and veg wholesaling business, my best friend and I set the business up as a partnership. Our accountant advised us to set it up as a limited company but we knew better – I'd been friends with my partner since school. It was fine until my so-called friend disappeared. I then discovered that he had spent thousands that we didn't have and I was liable for the debt.* ❞
– Larry Ford, Director, Larry the Fruit II

You might ask why this section is in a chapter called 'Have you got what it takes?'. It's because deciding the formal structure of your business has more to do with you, your motivation and what you want out of the business than with anything else. The way you structure the business should be a close reflection of the influences that are driving you to do it in the first place.

> Think about how you are going to structure the business before you start spending any money. You will be making a mistake if you let matters drift and find yourself in a position where circumstances and not your own drives are dictating the outcome.

You will need to think hard about the exact form of your business, partly for your own convenience but crucially because you will need to define the *legal* structure of your business and therefore the responsibilities that it and you have towards other individuals and companies you are associated with. If you are in any doubt take legal advice but in many circumstances the best structure is fairly obvious. The main forms of business are *sole trader*, *limited company* and *partnership*. Other options include *co-operatives* and *franchises*.

Sole trading

Sole trading is the simplest form of business, and the one that leaves you with the most control. You can put in as much money as you like and you are free to run the business as you like. But you are also entirely responsible for it and if the business fails you can go bust yourself. That means that the bank and other people you owe money to may have a claim against your house, your car, everything you own.

Partnership

Partnership is similarly relatively unregulated but you should think carefully about whether you need a partner, what that person will contribute – whether it be financial resources, special skills, a valuable network, or even just a personality that complements your own – and whether or not you want to share your profits with that person. Perhaps the most important aspect of partnership to bear in mind is that you will be 'jointly and severally' liable for all the partnership's debts. So if your partner incurs a debt, even if you know nothing about it, you will be responsible for it.

Limited companies

Many businesses are registered as private limited companies. The main advantage of these is that in law your company has an identity which is distinct from your own. It exists independently of you, so if the business fails you won't usually be personally liable.

Franchises

Franchises are different. You can take up a franchise as a sole trader, a limited company or a partnership and the great advantage is that you can run your own business with a product or service that is already successful, using the financial and marketing clout of a much larger organisation. Needless to say franchises are more popular with investors because of the relatively low failure rate. But it can go wrong so make sure that you:

- *talk to some of the company's existing franchisees*
- *check out the franchisor's management structure*
- *take a close look at its audited accounts*
- *examine its history in your area (or at least in a similar one).*

Pros and cons of business structures

	Pros	Cons
Sole trader	You can set up straight away, with no fuss and bureaucracy You have complete control so you can be as ambitious or cautious as you want	You are personally liable for all your debts You have no access to equity capital (which is relatively risk free)
Partnership	You share risk and investment You have a wider pool of skills, shared networks and are relatively unrestricted	You share the profits You are liable for all debts You will need to pay for a carefully drafted partnership agreement
Limited company	You aren't normally liable personally for debts The business image is better You will be a company director rather than a proprietor	More complex to set up Your power is restricted by the Articles of Association You will probably need more (and more expensive) professional advice
Co-operative	Profits are shared in proportion to input The business does not need to be run for financial gain	You have no more control of the business than any of your colleagues It may be difficult to attract investment
Franchise	You will probably need less money than would be needed to start up an equivalent business alone You can rely on the support, brands and reputation of a household name	The franchisor has a fair degree of control over your business You have to pay the franchisor

The key thing to bear in mind is that the structure of your business will define your legal responsibilities. Making the wrong decision could land you in a lot of trouble later on.

Know the likely pitfalls

> **"** *My business is a success now – seven years after starting up – but when I think of the time and money I could have saved just by*

thinking a bit about what could have gone wrong
before it did, I could cry. **99**
– Frans Petersen, Petersen Nanotechnology

Ask yourself the following questions:

○ **About you**: Are you the right kind of person to build a business?
Have you got an entrepreneur's personality? Have you got
experience in the business you are planning to grow? Have you
got a great network of potential customers, suppliers and
advisers? Can you sell yourself and your product or service?

○ **About your product or service**: Is it technically feasible? Do
people want it? Do you know who else is supplying it? Have you
checked out any possible legal or environmental objections? Very
few products or services continue for ever unchanged so have you
thought how you will develop it?

○ **About your market**: Have you analysed it properly (gut feeling is
all well and good but it's no substitute for proper research)? Have
you considered the cost of reaching it? Have you worked out how
much customers will be prepared to pay for your new offering? Do
you know how will you get them to trust you?

○ **About your business**: Is your head ruling your heart when it
comes to the structure of the business? Have you considered the
financial implications (more on this later)? Have you got personal
capital that you can put into the business? If not, are you prepared
to give up part of the business to raise capital? Have you assessed
your personal financial needs, how much you need to live?

Wherever you answer "no" there is a likely pitfall. Work systematically to convert each "no" into a resounding "yes". You may need
to draft in specialist advice (see next chapter) but you really do
need to cover all the ground if you are planning for success.

A final thought about your office. Are you going to be working
from home? If you are, think about what life might be like. Will
your children come home mid-afternoon and distract you? Will
your partner object to you turning a bedroom or a garage into a
huge filing cabinet? How close are you to a post office? Can you
cope with a diet of isolation and interruption? The simplest things
can make life miserable for homeworkers. But the commute is great.

Tips for budding entrepreneurs

Thinking carefully about yourself, your product or service and the
structure of your company is an essential first step towards going
into business for yourself.

Take an honest look at yourself:

1. Think about yourself as an entrepreneur. Try to put yourself in the shoes of a role model business person. Do they fit? What is your vision? What will the business look like in five years? If you can't come up with a convincing picture it could be that you aren't cut out for it.

2. Talk to successful business people you know and read profiles of great entrepreneurs. Have they got something you haven't? If it's only luck and being in the right place at the right time then there's nothing to stop you emulating them. (However, there *is* more to it than that!)

3. Take a business you know reasonably well – a local restaurant, for instance, or a taxi company that you use – and write down ten ways that the managers could improve it. Thinking about other businesses, even if they are entirely unrelated, can stimulate great ideas about your own.

4. You may need to pay yourself as little as possible in the very early stages. Calculate your domestic expenditure in the last three months. Exactly where is your money going? What are you prepared to sacrifice? Work out what you actually **need**, but add in a contingency amount to take account of those sudden unforeseen bills.

What's in this chapter for you

Decide what help you need . . .
. . . and when you will need it
Get the most out of legal and financial advice
Know what other help is there for you

❝ *We used an accountant right from the outset – basically, when we were just playing around with the business. She was brilliant – she helped us to understand finance and book-keeping, recommended financial management software programs, helped us set up a presentation to the bank. She even found our offices for us!* ❞
– Kevin Cross, Fish merchant

Decide what help you need . . .

❝ *I made the mistake early on of asking a lawyer for a general chat about my proposed business. When I saw the bill I realised that I wasn't going to make that mistake twice!* ❞
– Graham Black, Business communications consultant

You *will* need professional advice and unfortunately this will cost money. However it will be money well spent if you follow some simple rules. This chapter is about how to get the most for the least.

> Think about the skills you have and compare them with the skills you know you will need. The first thing to do is to accept that you will need help in some areas.

By now you should have identified some gaps in your knowledge, experience or temperament. Don't worry about them – the key thing is that you know they are there. People who develop great businesses rarely have detailed knowledge of finance, marketing, accounting, finance and insurance, the law, public relations and the rest of the mix that makes up a business.

It's easy to fall into the trap of thinking that getting professional

ACT!

> Draw up a checklist of all the areas of business where you are not confident that you have all the expertise you will need.
>
> ☐ *Technical?*
> ☐ *Marketing?*
> ☐ *Sales (at home and abroad)?*
> ☐ *Managerial?*
> ☐ *Financial?*
> ☐ *Other?*
>
> Now plug the gaps by sourcing professional advice.

advice is throwing money down the drain, on the one hand, and a waste of your valuable time on the other. After all, you didn't select the swashbuckling life of the entrepreneur to sit in an accountant's office for hours!

In fact most businesses actually *profit* from the advice of lawyers, accountants, bankers and consultants.

> **“** *Our accountant spent a day with us recently. She came in to check the books generally, and to make sure we were using the software correctly. After looking at them for a few minutes she gave us two pieces of advice that we could implement that day which saved us 10 per cent of our annual revenue. Or to put it another way, in one day she contributed 80 times her annual fee to our business. And no, I'm not telling you what her advice was!* **”**
> **– Graham Black**

So, accountants can be good for you!

. . . and when you will need it

> **“** *Never underestimate your need for help in the six months or so before your business takes off!* **”**
> **– Bernard Carr, Big City Training**

You will need sound advice throughout the life of your business, but you need it most of all before the business even starts. You will need to choose your bank, solicitor and accountant before you begin to operate just to get yourself technically off the ground. But look at your checklist of professional needs and start to fill in the gaps. For instance, if you are a bit hazy about public relations, but you know that your new product will need a lot of favourable press coverage from the outset, you need to plug this gap *before* you draft your business plan. A venture capitalist or bank manager will be quick to punch holes in your plans if a key area of expertise isn't properly accounted for.

> **"** *Our financial training courses were technically brilliant, but our backer pointed out that none of us had teaching or presentation skills! We bought a week's worth of a communications consultant's time before we started. It wasn't cheap but it was the best investment we've made in the ten year history of the business.* **"**
> **– Bernard Carr**

As the business grows you will need more advice rather than less. Conventional wisdom is that you need most professional help during the three critical phases of the business – birth, growth and death (don't forget that 'death' can mean making your personal fortune by selling out for a very large amount of money!). In reality though you would do well to keep your professional advisers very much in touch with your business throughout its life.

Draw up a list of specific solicitors, accountants and so on. Ask friends, colleagues, even competitors, which companies they use, and why. Contact them all for details of their services and whittle down the list to two or three of each type. Arrange appointments with them, BUT *don't actually visit them before you read the next section!* ·

Get the most out of legal and financial advice

> **"** *Once I realised that my bank manager has his own business to run I was able to develop a real rapport with him. We chat about once a week but the relationship delivers much more value to the business than it first appears, because there is such a constant flow of good advice.* **"**
> **– Wendy Hole, Hole Wholefoods**

Think about the real information and advice you need from each of your professional advisers. A surprising amount of free information is available from government agencies, libraries and Chambers of Commerce. It's a lot cheaper to work through a manual to understand your financial management software than it is to have your accountant spend a day talking you through it!

The first key to getting the most out of expensive professional advice is to know exactly what it is that you need to know. The second key is to remember that your advisers are running businesses too – they are going to charge you for every minute of their time that you consume. The third key is to acknowledge that they could be in and around your business for a very long time and so your personal relations need to be good. The chemistry between adviser and the advised is important. Mutual trust and understanding take a while to develop but you have to believe from the outset that the potential for such a relationship is there.

Make a list of the specific questions to which you need answers. Check them. Ask yourself if there is a more cost effective way of getting the information you need. Share the list with friends who might be able to direct you to good sources of advice.

BUT *don't accept amateur advice on critical issues such as the law, raising finance and insurance, for instance.*

Accountants *must* be able to write up and audit your year-end accounts, but they *should* be able to advise you on your book-keeping system, help you do some forecasting, handle your pay roll, advise on the best company structure for you and point you towards cash-raising opportunities, including government grants. One firm should be able to advise you on all these issues. Try to keep as much as possible under one roof, and if possible with one contact person.

Your lawyer should be able to advise on employment law and

other contracts, debt collection, negotiating leases on business premises and, particularly, drawing up the 'rules' of your business, whether it is a partnership agreement or a limited company's Memorandum and Articles of Association.

Your bank manager is likely to be key to your enterprise. You will probably need the full range of banking facilities whether or not you are borrowing from the bank to develop your business. Most banks offer broadly comparable services and broadly comparable costs, so here more than elsewhere your relationship with the manager might be the deciding factor. A sympathetic bank manager can make a big difference to your business and your peace of mind. But never forget that they are in business too!

These three sources of professional advice do overlap a little in the services they provide. Make sure you are not duplicating effort and cost!

Know what other advice is out there for you

❝ *There's a bewildering array of advisers and consultants out there.* **❞**
– Wendy Hole

It's true. There is. Some kinds of advice you may need to seek at a fairly early stage, probably at the suggestion of one or more of your primary advisers, concern property, insurance and marketing.

You might think all this is pretty boring, but the consequences of under-insurance, for example, can be bankruptcy or liquidation. All businesses are obliged by law to have general insurance against theft, fire and accident and so on, but you may also be well-advised to consider key-man insurance, professional liability and product and public liability, depending on the sort of business you are in. A couple of things to check out when selecting an insurance adviser are the small print of his policy (make sure you are getting what you think you are getting) and his track record as far as claims payment is concerned.

If you need premises you may be recommended certain estate agents, architects and surveyors. Professional circles can be quite intricately interconnected. Don't be surprised to find close links between certain bank managers, solicitors, accountants, estate agents and insurance advisers. The social chains can be very strong. Use them!

Then there is the multitude of marketing, training and financial consultants all looking to help you along. International sales may be an issue to consider early on. If you are planning to export you will need to set up an agency network. You may need help to get the right agents.

Tips for dealing with advisers

It is vital to know exactly what you want before you even start talking to any potential adviser.

Get the best from advisers:

1. Always meet the person in the practice who you will be dealing with.
2. Don't ask professionals to sort out matters you can deal with yourself.
3. If they don't act quickly and return your calls you're off to a bad start. Don't put up with it!
4. Make sure that the firms you select can deal with every type of issue your business might face.
5. Cost professional advice as closely as you can. Make sure you've got a good idea of how often you will be consulting them and how much you will be charged for the privilege.
6. Always make sure that when you come out of a meeting with your advisers you fully understand the advice you have been given. You are paying for it, after all, and clarification later may be costly.
7. Choose an accountant appropriate for your size and check that he or she has a knowledge of your particular line of business.

What's in this chapter for you

Understand the marketing mix
Develop a marketing plan
Decide your sales tactics
Fine tune your distribution

> ❝ *Some of my friends have done MBA courses and when they talk to me about marketing I wonder if we're speaking the same language; they make it seem so complicated. I've since learnt that it's mainly common sense. Ninety per cent of it is simply reversing the act of being a customer.* ❞
> **– Jack Kay, Market gardener**

Understand the marketing mix

> ❝ *I find it much more rewarding to look at life through the eyes of my customers than through the eyes of my broccoli!* ❞
> **– Jack Kay**

What Jack means is that if you view your business through the eyes and experiences of your customer you won't go far wrong. Jack's 90 per cent right. But the other 10 per cent is pretty important, especially if it is not dressed up in marketing babble. It's the 10 per cent of useful theory that allows you to build the bigger market picture and establish the framework for your marketing strategy, even if you don't call it that.

One very basic marketing model is the 4Ps of the marketing mix – product, price, place and promotion.

Ask yourself four simple questions to understand the marketing mix:

- ❑ *How will customers benefit from your Product (or service)?*
- ❑ *How important will Price be to them?*
- ❑ *Where will you sell it to them – what is the Place of the transaction?*
- ❑ *How will you Promote it to them?*

Product

Put yourself in the position of your customer and think about the product or service you are offering. Don't think about what it *is*, about how well made it is and the many useful features. Think about what it *does*. What do all those features, for instance, really deliver to the people who are using them?

The publisher of the 60 Minutes series of books, for instance, carefully designed the structure of the books to ensure that each delivers a genuinely improved learning experience. The customer benefit is enhanced absorption of information.

> Take a dispassionate look at what you are offering:
>
> ☐ *Draw up a list of the qualities or features of your product or service which you most prize.*
> ☐ *Now write next to them the benefit to the customer of each one.*

You need to think quite carefully about this as the real benefit is not always the obvious one. The customer benefit of, say, a lawnmower, to take a very simple example, is *not* that it cuts grass. The customer benefit is a tidy garden. See the difference? Don't think of your customers as static. The customer benefit of a television set to a harassed parent is not quality programming. It is quiet, occupied children. A few hours later the very same customer may be looking for a different benefit. Credit card companies know that a significant segment of their customer base is less interested in a credit facility than in making a statement about themselves by using a certain type of card. You need to try to get into the lives of your customer.

> Spend an hour running through a day in the life of one of your customers. Where does your product come into it? How will *you* make a difference to that day?

Price

Price is often not as important a factor in the purchasing decision as you may think. Ask the manufacturers of premium beers, for instance, or fashion designers!

List your competitors' products and their prices. How do they compare with yours? Remember two things.

1. It is not *necessarily* better to be lower priced. If you are delivering a superior customer experience you can charge more.
2. Don't think of your competitors as only the makers or suppliers of products or services similar to your own. Your competitors could include anyone who wants your customer's money. Your customers are individuals. Think of a person who wants to buy a new BMW this year but who also really needs to move to a more expensive house. For budgetary reasons she can't do both. Who is BMW's competitor? Saab? Audi? No, it's a tiny village estate agent.

The price you set for your product or service needs to do a number of things. First of all it needs to deliver a profit margin to you. Think about all the costs you will incur and calculate the margin. You are likely to need at least 40 per cent if you are to cover your overheads and have enough left to develop and expand the business. Secondly it is an important part of your story in the market. What does your price say to customers? What image do you want to portray? Budget? Luxury? Value? Premium? Think about the words you want to come into your customers' minds when they think of your business. Of course in some markets and industries this is inappropriate. If you are selling bridges to developing countries words like 'luxury' have little meaning.

> ❝ *I started an up-market florist business last year, providing exotic foliage for a wealthy clientele. My prices matched those of standard retail florists and my flowers were much more unusual and in far*

better condition. I thought I couldn't lose, yet customers wouldn't switch to me. I did some research and trebled my prices. It turned out that my customers weren't interested in 'value'. They wanted exclusivity. That insight marked the point when business really started to boom. **99**

– Tim Burgess, Exotic Blooms

Place

You should think carefully about the 'place' where you will trade with your customers. If you are a retailer think about where people will want to buy your product or service. Can you charge a premium by delivering more convenience? You will probably pay a little bit more for the eggs you buy at the petrol station as you fill up on the way home, but it's worth a few pence not to have to stop again and queue at a supermarket. But there are plenty of other 'places' to sell – on the Internet, for instance, or door-to-door, by direct mail or to wholesalers. The principle is the same – look at 'place' decisions from your customers' perspective. Many marketing innovations have come from challenging conventional wisdom about the place of trade. Look at TV shopping or the changes in the retail banking sector!

Promotion

And finally there is promotion. The aim of promotion is to:

- ○ *Tell potential customers that you exist.*
- ○ *Explain to them what you are selling and what the benefits to them are.*
- ○ *Persuade them that yours is a better overall package of benefits than any other available offer.*
- ○ *Persuade them to repeat their order and become loyal to your brand.*

Think about the last item you bought. Why did you buy it? What were the factors in the package that persuaded you to buy that particular item? Will you buy it again? If not, why not?

You should consider the various promotional vehicles as well as the message you are putting across. Some media are inappropriate for carrying certain messages. You don't often find milk advertised in up-market country magazines, and not many fridge freezers are sold door-to-door!

Which of the following promotional vehicles are suitable for your product or service?

- ❏ TV advertising
- ❏ Newspaper advertising (local or national – big difference)
- ❏ Specialist magazine advertising
- ❏ Inserts in newspapers or magazines
- ❏ Mail order
- ❏ Door-to-door leafleting
- ❏ Advertising in Yellow Pages
- ❏ Telesales
- ❏ Billboard posters
- ❏ Radio advertising
- ❏ Advertising on taxis or buses
- ❏ Press coverage . . .

The list is endless. Think about where your customers are when they are thinking about what it is you are selling. It's not really surprising that beer commercials feature strongly during major televised sporting events is it?

Develop a marketing plan

> ❝ I worked on a framework using the 4Ps and then I sat down to write a marketing plan . . . but I just couldn't. I had never written a marketing plan before and I was confused by the jargon. I became really worried. Then a friend told me it didn't matter – the real work was in thinking about all the options and deciding what my product really would mean to customers. The plan was in my head, almost at an intuitive level, although I **had** done all the necessary research. I really **understood** my own story. ❞
> **– Bill Kitson, Conference organiser**

Marketing plans needn't be PhD theses. They don't even need to be written down, but they do need to exist, if only in the minds and behaviour of everyone in the business.

List the promotional activities that you intend to undertake.

❑ *Work out when in your overall campaign you will undertake them (remember you don't have to do everything on day one).*
❑ *Work out how much each will cost.*
❑ *Now try to work out what effect it will all have on sales.*
❑ *Calculate if you can afford to do it all – what would you sacrifice if not?*
❑ *What are the cash implications of promoting ahead of receiving money from your sales?*

You will need a marketing plan as part of your overall business plan if you are looking for financial backing. Potential investors will want to see strong evidence of the positive impact your marketing will have, and of course they will want to see how much it will cost.

Decide your sales tactics

❝ *I used to think sales was mainly about grinning a lot and wearing a suit. But when you run your own business it is part of your life.* ❞
– Frans Peterson

Selling is an important subset of marketing and it needs to be considered separately.

Ask a friend or colleague to help you with this. Look around the room you are in right now. Choose an object. It doesn't matter whether its a painting or a pencil sharpener, a cycle helmet or a drawing pin – someone, somewhere has sold it.

Now sell it to your companion. Don't think too hard about it – just let it flow.

The tactics you will need if you are planning a nationwide garden greenhouse business are very different from those of, say, a building contractor with just two very large customers. But for both there is a useful framework used by sales professionals everywhere. It can really help to order your thoughts and discipline your conversation with a potential customer if you think of it as a sequence of stages:

○ Find out about your prospective customer's life. How is it structured? Who approves buying decisions? Is your prospective customer **really** a prospective customer – or does he or she have to refer to someone else?
○ Find out what your customer **needs**. Don't think of him as Mr Prospect. Think of him as someone you can help. If you understand his business problem or his domestic need, however small, you will be able to show more effectively how your particular product or service might provide the answer.
○ Handle the objections, don't be frightened by them. Use objections to your advantage. It is a lot easier to sell to people who voice their concerns than to those who don't. An objection is an opportunity – though it might not always seem that way!
○ Ask for the order! Sales professionals talk about 'closing the sale'. It's easy to see what they mean but it can be misleading. A good 'closed' sale is in fact one that is 'open' for the rest of the life of your business.

Remember that telephone (or whatever) that you just tried to sell to your friend. Try it again using the stages of a sales call as above. Spend a few minutes first thinking about your friend's need, how your particular telephone set can solve it, what her objections might be and how you would handle them.
  Easier second time round?

Fine tune your distribution

❝ My business was fashionable luxury bedroom furniture for kids up to the age of about 12. I opened a couple of shops which did quite well. But my business really exploded when I set up displays in play groups in up-market parts of the city and gave the owners a commission on sales they took there and then. It was great because wealthy parents were seeing my furniture at the moment that they were most tuned in to their kids and their kids' needs. ❞
– Sue Tow, Kids' Stuff Furnishings

Many of the decisions affecting your distribution will already be determined by the type of business you are in. If you are a retailer your shops are likely to be your main distribution channel. But even then you could have other channels – mail order for instance.

The main distribution channels are:

○ *Retail outlets (can be hypermarkets, corner shops, stalls in a market, post offices, petrol stations, specialist shops, banks ... don't get locked into a particular mindset – think about alternative retail outlets to those used by your competitors).*
○ *Mail order (can be coupon advertisements in newspapers and magazines, or catalogue and leaflet mailings direct to customers' addresses).*
○ *Door-to-door (if it's right for your business do it – don't be put off by the image!).*
○ *Wholesalers (hold very large volumes of stock, usually for small retailers).*
○ *Party plan ('parties' in which agents demonstrate products to friends and relatives, and then beyond to other groups).*

ACT!

Think about the advantages and disadvantages of the different distribution channels for your particular product or service. You need to weigh up:

❑ *The capital implications – for instance mail order can be a higher margin channel for you if it helps you avoid expensive high street premises.*
❑ *What the market wants – people are not going to want to buy houses, say, by mail order.*
❑ *The cost implications – a full-page coupon advertisement in a national tabloid newspaper is very expensive, but so is employing a field sales team.*

The important issues to keep in mind when thinking about distribution are:

○ *meeting the needs of customers;*
○ *generating the right volume of sales; and*
○ *the capital and cash implications.*

Tips for Failsafe Marketing

If you get the marketing right, your business will have the best possible foundations.

The key to success is to know your customers and understand how your product or service satisfies *their* needs – not yours.

1. Try to 'shadow' a customer ... literally, if possible, (without exposing yourself to a charge of stalking!) or in your imagination, if not. Build a profile of him or her and work out where your product or service fits in.

2. Select one of your competitors and try to do some business with them. How does it feel? What are they getting right for you? What could be improved? Your aim should be to find what you could do better than them.

3. Ask some potential customers to evaluate your competitors' services or products. Try to find out what would happen to sales if they doubled their price...or halved it. Use this to refine your own pricing policy.

4. Assess how you can best promote your product or service. Should you advertise or would it be more appropriate to meet your customers face to face, or both?

5. Analyse where and how your customers will buy your product and choose the most suitable distribution channel to match. Do you need a retail outlet or will you sell door-to-door? Or would mail order or party plans be best?

6. If you are not a natural salesperson consider taking a course. Even if you won't be selling your product or service directly yourself, you will need to be able to sell it to your representatives.

What's in this chapter for you

Get a grip on the records you need to keep
Peer into your financial future
Understand the tax system
Learn how to control overheads

> " *I learnt the hard way that continuously making and selling things can give you a false sense of security. I didn't spend enough time on cash and profit because I thought it must be looking good. I was selling so much. After eight months I was into a massive rescue mission, and it didn't need to happen.* "
> **– Richard Beare, Pots Galore**

Get a grip on the records you need to keep

> " *Of the four of us who started the business only one had any sense of how to keep financial records. When he was away from the office following an accident we didn't have a clue what was going on. It set us back months. You should always have more than one person monitoring the financial health of the business.* "
> **– Don Jenkins, Printer**

Many businesses fail, and most of the ones that do fail do so as a direct consequence of poor financial controls. You have to be in a position to take action immediately when your business looks as though it is running into problems. And you can't possibly do that unless you have up-to-the-minute records of where your business is right now.

Have you got your head around the financial issues? Think about which areas of the business you will need most financial information about. What's going to keep you awake at night?

How did you get on? Your list of financial priorities will reflect your temperament, skills and the nature of your industry and business. But it should contain the following five key elements of effective financial control. You must know:

○ *Your exact current financial position – you need regular data about your business. You can't rely on your annual accounts!*
○ *Your forecast position for the next few months – so you can see how income and outgoings are stacking up and head off any problems early on.*
○ *The position you need to be in to meet budgets – you will need to amend short-term profit and cashflow forecasts.*
○ *What actions are available to you – you need to understand the implications of taking any particular route to avoid problems.*
○ *How effective your action has been – you need to be able to review the performance of your business and learn from it.*

You can't know any of this unless you keep good financial records. If you aren't going to be keeping these records yourself make sure that someone else is! You can bring in part-time book-keeping services easily – don't assume that it's all a matter of having a good memory.

At its most basic, records will tell you how much money you owe and how much you are owed. This will help you to:

○ *improve your financial control*
○ *spot rising costs that are damaging your margins*
○ *measure your overall performance*
○ *manage your cashflow properly*
○ *act quickly if the need arises.*

You might be turned off by the thought of book-keeping but be in no doubt that up-to-date financial records can save your business from potential disaster!

It's worth looking at the growing range of computer programs which will look after your accounts. The right package could take the pain out of staying in touch.

Peer into your financial future

❝ When I told my bank manager that it's impossible to plan the future of the fortune telling business he thought I was trying to be funny. But it's true! ❞
– Gypsy Mary Mee, Fortune teller

We've all heard people say that in *their* type of business you can't plan, you can't look into the future, it's just too unpredictable. Sadly it's not as easy as that. Planning is not an issue you can avoid. You have to plan so you can raise capital on the one hand, and manage your business on the other.

The main mechanisms for looking at the future are the cash flow and sales forecasts, the balance sheet and profit and loss account.

Divide the next year into twelve monthly periods. Write down how many units you think you will sell in each month.

You will need to bear in mind seasonal factors. Do people want to buy more or less of your type of product or service in August when they may be on holiday, or in December during the run up to Christmas? Will sales be dependent on any regular seismic social shifts such as the movement of hundreds of thousands of students in September and October? Will your business be affected by the weather? Will your prices fluctuate during this period or will they remain static? If they do change what effect will that have on unit sales?

Now try the same exercise for a three year period. This is the basis of your cashflow projection.

The balance sheet is a statement of the assets and liabilities of the business at any one time. It's often referred to as a 'snap-shot' of the business because it takes a fixed point (usually the end of the financial year) and shows where the money to fund the business came from, and where it was spent. It is an overview of what the business owns, such as fixed assets (e.g. machinery or computers, land or buildings, items that you use within the business and wouldn't normally sell). It will also account for stocks, cash in the bank and debtors (people or businesses who owe you money). Finally, it will account the 'liabilities' of the business such as loans, trade creditors and share capital.

Unlike the balance sheet the profit and loss is a moving picture. Put simply, the P&L will tell you if you if you are selling whatever it is you provide for more or less than it costs to get it to the person who is paying for it.

List all the sources of your revenues and costs. Start at the top with sources of revenue – these include income from sales, owners' capital, other capital introduced and loans.

Now list all your direct costs – these are the expenses you incur, such as materials and labour, which vary according to the number of units you produce or services you provide (they're sometimes called variable costs). For example the publisher of this book will include as direct costs items such as paper and printing costs, the commission he pays to his sales force, distribution costs and the author's royalty – all things which vary according to the number of books he makes and sells.

If you take your total direct costs from your revenues you are left with your 'gross profit'.

Now list all your indirect or fixed costs. Basically these are all your overheads, all the costs of running your business that you wouldn't normally allocate to a specific product or activity – your rent, postage, stationery, salaries and so on.

Take the total indirect costs from the gross profit and you have your 'trading profit', or PBIT (profit before interest and tax).

With all this information you can begin to project revenues, and the costs you will incur, and gradually build up a cashflow forecast. It is very important to remember that making a sale is not the same as receiving the money for it in your bank account (just as you could buy something without paying for it immediately).

Think about the credit you will be extending to customers. Will different types of customer enjoy different credit periods? When will customers in other countries be paying you? What about the credit extended to you by your suppliers? Do you think it will match the credit you are giving so that money goes in and out of your account at around the same time?

Cashflow is often more important than short-term profit. Profit takes account of the figures, but cashflow takes account of the figures *and* the timing of cash receipts and payments.

> Think about the impact on your business if all your P&L
> calculations proved to be absolutely spot on, but the cashflow
> shows all your cash turning up six months later than you
> forecast.
>
> Actually you don't need to think too hard. Unless you've got
> very deep pockets you'll be out of business!

Profit is, of course, central to any business so any action taken to
improve it will eventually affect cashflow too. But there are steps
you can take to improve cashflow regardless of profit:

○ *Encourage your customers to pay promptly (but don't offer prompt
settlement discounts unless the cost of discount is lower than the
cost of, say, borrowing from the bank).*
○ *Take the maximum available credit from your suppliers (but don't
get a reputation for late payment – stick to the rules).*
○ *Reduce your stock levels (if they are unnecessarily high).*
○ *Pay for your fixed assets over time, or lease them, rather than
paying cash up front.*

Understand the tax system

> ❝ *I thought tax was something our accountants would sort out,
> until our first VAT assessment nearly killed us!* ❞
> **– Sue Batham, Travel specialist**

Obviously if you've got effective financial controls on your
business you greatly increase your chances of success. But
remember that increased success brings increased responsibilities,
especially towards the taxman! Your accountant will guide you
through the intricacies of the tax system, but you should have a
grasp of the basic principles so that you can minimise the amount
of tax you pay.

There a several taxes on individuals and businesses and you
would be well advised to do a little research on the implications
of each of them for you and your business. The three fundamental
types of tax are:

○ *Direct taxes on income and profits (e.g. Income Tax and National
Insurance, Corporation Tax)*

○ *Taxes on capital (Capital Gains Tax and Inheritance Tax)*
○ *Indirect taxes (Customs and Excise Duties, and VAT).*

If you operate as a sole trader you will pay normal rates of Income Tax on your profits (including the salary you pay yourself). If you are in a partnership the amount of Income Tax charged on profits will depend on the Income Tax rates paid by the individual partners on their income. If you operate as a limited company you will pay income tax on your salary at normal prevailing rates. Any profits left in the business will be liable for Corporation Tax. Naturally it is important for company directors to think hard about tactics for minimising Corporation Tax.

If you are a director *and* a shareholder you should think carefully about balancing the money taken out of the company between salary, dividends and possibly a company pension plan. As always, take professional advice before committing yourself.

If you are going to be employing other people the PAYE scheme dictates that you will have to collect their Income Tax and National Insurance contributions. In addition you will need to pay the employer's contribution towards your employees' National Insurance.

Capital Gains Tax is levied on sales of some fixed assets (a building for instance). The important thing to remember is that if you replace the fixed asset (buy another building) assessment of capital gains may be postponed.

Think about your business in terms of your likely tax liabilities. Too boring? An unexpected tax bill can destroy a growing business. You owe it to yourself, your staff, your advisers and all the people who have supported you to know exactly which taxes you will face. Sue Batham's experience is not uncommon!

Once you know what you will be expected to pay you can ask your accountant to advise you on ways of paying the minimum.

Learn how to control overheads

> **"** *I couldn't believe the impact that firing everyone had on the bottom line. I only wish I could do it again!* **"**
> **– Ronnie Bickerstaff, Tod Sloan Publishing**

Take a look at your P&L again. Look at your fixed costs in particular. Which are the real drains on your profitability?

Try to think creatively of ways to reduce your biggest fixed costs. Which are the big ones?

❏ *Wages and salaries? Can you do more with fewer people on the payroll? Can you pay yourself less? Would investment in technology have so beneficial an effect on your payroll that your overall costs are lower? Can you use more freelance services as Ronnie did?*
❏ *Marketing? Reassess your advertising budget perhaps? Spend three months concentrating on press coverage rather display advertisements?*
❏ *Travel and subsistence? Postpone that two week research trip to Bali for a few months?*

Chances are two or three sources of cost will dominate. It's the old 80:20 principle in operation. Something like 20 per cent of the lines in your list of fixed costs will account for 80 per cent of the overall spend. So concentrate your energy on the costs that are making the big difference.

Remember that in an expanding business – and that's what you want – overheads are bound to increase. The situation to look out for is when overheads are going up when expressed as a percentage of sales. Taking on three or four new members of staff is fine, but you need a corresponding increase in revenue. If sales don't jump, your margins will be badly squeezed.

Tips for rock-solid financial control

Firm control of finances is the backbone of any successful enterprise.

With an up-to-the-minute picture of your income and outgoings, you should be able to maintain the health of your business.

1. Write up your records regularly – don't allow invoices and receipts to collect in an old cardboard box on a shelf waiting for the ledger fairy to sort things out for you. If you can't do it yourself, there are plenty of freelance book-keepers who could help you.

2. There are many ready-made record systems available and some very good computer software. Check them out – you don't have to reinvent double entry book-keeping.

3. It's worth paying for some advice in this area. If your records get muddled it can be a nightmare to sort them out.

4. Not surprisingly, profitability can be destroyed if you don't maintain a firm grip on your outgoings. If your business is expanding it's vital to check that your overheads are not rising in percentage terms when compared with sales.

5. As soon as you start working on your own account inform the tax authorities. Make sure you understand fully which taxes you will be liable for and ensure you have enough money put away to cover them.

6. Be aware of any 'penalties' imposed by revenue authorities for failure to maintain and retain proper business financial records.

7. Remember: you must file accounts and tax returns by the date prescribed by law.

What's in this chapter for you

Know all the sources of potential finance
Calculate how much money you will need . . .
. . . and when you will need it
Weigh up the pros and cons

❝ *I knew I had a great business idea. Just knew it. My business plan was perfect but after just five minutes with a venture capitalist I realised that I was going to have to go back to the drawing board. She saw into problems I had never dreamed of. But eight months later when I went back to her with a new improved plan I got three times as much start up capital as I originally asked for.* ❞
– Stewart Hignett, Magazine publisher

Know all the sources of potential finance

❝ *The librarian at my city library became my best friend for the months before we started up! He knew an amazing amount about sources of business information.* ❞
– Stewart Hignett

You've got all your figures in spreadsheets and research findings and notes on different bits of paper, but before you can bring it all together into the grand plan you need to have some idea of who you will be asking for money from.

Ask yourself a few questions before your bank manager does!

❑ *How much money are you going to need? Don't just think about what you need to buy the equipment you want. Look at your cashflow forecasts and think about the working capital you will need. Many businesses that fail do so because they're undercapitalised.*

❑ *When are you going to need it? You may not need to take it all at the outset and if you can stagger the financing it may save you a lot of interest repayment.*

❑ *What do you need it for? You will have to explain to your backers exactly how their money is going to be used.*

❑ *What are you prepared to give in return? This is often the big question. You are unlikely to get finance for nothing and you need to think about what you are prepared to sacrifice – the security of your house? Equity in the business? Very high interest repayments?*

It's well worth researching the various sources of finance that might be available to you. Most people think of the high street banks as an obvious source, but there are also venture capitalists, business angels, government loans and grants, flotation on a stock market, customers and suppliers, remortgaging your home, redundancy money and so on. And don't forget what might be the cheapest form of financing around (although it may be the most emotionally taxing), your friends and family. At the end of this chapter we will weigh up the pros and cons of each.

Go to your local library. Many have business reference sections which will point you in the direction for further advice. They may also have details of 'free money' from government agencies, charities and so forth.

Calculate how much money you will need . . .

> ❝ *When I started my international steel business in Jakarta the outgoings and revenue were just incalculable. My way of financing it was to secure a massive first order before I spent anything. It wasn't quite as simple as this but the proceeds from that sale let me develop the business without incurring much long-term debt.* ❞
> **– Alexander Miles, Steel merchant**

If you have already listed all the costs associated with running your business you can start to calculate the total fixed costs. If not, now is as good a time as any! Start getting quotes for machinery you will require, cars and vans, computers and other office equipment, and you can plug some real figures into your spreadsheet. Try to go through each line systematically, getting real figures to replace your guesstimates. And make sure you cover all the angles. Do the quotes you are getting include VAT and service and installation costs? Don't forget the cost of insuring them either, or of the training courses or books you may need to run your equipment.

Beyond start up capital you will also need capital to run the business, working capital. Basically the working capital you will need at any given moment depends on two factors:

○ *the time it takes for your cash to turn into whatever it is you are selling and then back into cash again, and*
○ *your sales levels.*

The longer the cash-to-stock/service-to-cash cycle and the higher the level of your sales, the more working capital you need.

Take some time to plot the movement of a chunk of cash through your business. How long does it take to convert from cash in your bank account to something that you can sell. And if it's goods you are manufacturing, how long will that converted cash sit in a warehouse? And once it has sold, how long will it take to convert back to cash in your account?

A good rule of thumb when you have worked out how much investment you need is to add 25 per cent as a contingency fund. Undercapitalisation is a real source of individual and business stress.

. . . and when you will need it

❝ *Our financing was part debt and part equity. A venture capitalist gave us a substantial amount of money for a substantial share of the business, but he also made available to us an equivalent sum in the form of a high-interest loan. That has given us the flexibility to draw down the loan in chunks so minimising the interest we need to pay. We're now reaching the stage where we would like to replace some of the high-interest loan with cheaper money, so we are talking to all of the High Street banks.* ❞
– Jaques Low, Architect

By definition you will need all your start-up costs to be met at the start of your business, or very soon afterwards. But you may be able to be more flexible with your working capital, particularly if your business is going to be subject to large seasonal fluctuations. It's back to the cashflow forecasts. In order to calculate them properly you will need to have made some assumptions about the credit you will be giving and receiving.

Try to complete the following table. Some suggested answers have been added to guide you.

	Timing assumption	VAT to be added
Salaries		
Buy/make	30 days from invoice	Yes
Packaging		
Rent		
Rates		
Water		
Insurance		
Repairs/renewals		
Heat/light/power	Paid quarterly, in arrears	Yes
Postage	Due monthly	No
Printing/stationery		
Travel		
Telephone		
Professional fees		
Capital introduced		
Equipment repayments		
Accountancy fees		
Expenses		
VAT		

Your cashflow forecast will show you the bulges in the year when the demands on your cash resources outstrip the supply. These may be best dealt with by relatively cheap capital such as a bank overdraft or, even more cheaply, by using other people's money by extending your trade credit from suppliers. Another option is factoring. You may be able to get up to 80 per cent of the value of your credit sales *as soon as you make the sale* from a factoring agency. They will forward the remaining 20 per cent (less their fee) when the debt is finally collected.

> ❝ *Factoring was great for our business at the beginning, but less satisfying as we grew. We would recommend that any new business consider it though.* ❞
> **– William Blakey, Software manufacturer**

The other "when?" question relates to some of the fixed assets. If you don't need to buy and own them outright from the beginning you might consider hire-purchase or leasing. This will spread your outgoings in a predictable way and allow you to use the working capital you have released for something else. The overall cost to you of the vehicle or machinery may be higher than if you were to purchase it outright, but it may well be a cheaper way of financing the business than a bank loan for example.

Factoring, creditors and bank overdrafts are generally better sources of short-term finance, for instance, for stock, raw materials and debtors. Look to loans, mortgages and equity capital for financing of fixed assets and your longer-term working capital requirements.

Weigh up the pros and cons

> ❝ *You've just got to take professional advice when it gets down to a decision about financing your dream. The trouble is some professional advice comes with vested interests attached! In the end my three partners and I sorted it out with our accountant. We decided that if we were going to do it properly we would need a lot of money, and we recognised that we would have to give up some equity in the business to secure it. But we negotiated good share option incentives and now the four of us own 60 per cent of a £24 million business. I don't think we would have got this far on an overdraft!* ❞
> **– Darren Hardball, Fashion designer**

So you are likely to end up with a combination of sources of finance. (Even if you are starting fairly modestly, say with a redundancy payment, you are still likely to need a bank overdraft at times, and you will almost certainly have a credit arrangement with key suppliers.) But the precise combination will depend on the circumstances of your business.

There are advantages and drawbacks to each method of finance.

Bank loans and overdrafts

Banks are, of course, the most experienced lenders to new businesses and are the major source of finance for start-ups. As with any investor though they don't automatically lend money, and your plans will need to be very solid if you are to convince your bank manager to back you. You may be asked to match from your own resources the amount that you are asking the bank to provide, and you will almost certainly be asked to provide some security against the loan – your house, or shares, or life policies for instance. And don't forget that you have to pay the loan back, so you should schedule that into your cash forecasts. Interest rates vary so it pays to shop around, but one of the attractions of a bank advance is the more personal relationship you can have. So keep that in mind when comparing rates – is the personal chemistry right?

Overdrafts are a simple form of short-term finance. They are ideal for covering temporary cash shortages but not for buying, say, a new fleet of trucks! You don't want to be too exposed either. If the bank decides to call in the overdraft it can put you out of business if you can't rapidly convert stock and debtors into cash to pay it off.

> **"** *Don't get carried away with an overdraft facility – it isn't free!* **"**
> **– Darren Hardball**

Venture capital

There is a very large network of individuals (sometimes called 'business angels') and organisations whose business it is to spot and inject large amounts of capital into promising investments. The catch? They require correspondingly large amounts of equity.

Venture capital companies tend not to invest in start-up businesses because of their relatively high failure rate. They will usually demand a substantial equity share and some control of (or at least say in) the way the business is run. And they may want a very quick exit, which may not suit you. Business angels may be a better bet if you are in a start-up situation and are prepared to part with some of your business. They can bring useful skills and experience along with their investment – but you have to feel that you can work with them. Your accountant may know of a local network of private investors.

> ❝ *If your angel is only an 'angel' as long as he isn't making suggestions about the business you won't be partners for long – and remember, it's his bat and his ball you're playing with.* ❞
> **– Rupert Blackwall, Business angel**

Grants

Depending on your business circumstances you may be eligible for grants from charities or government departments. Obviously there aren't many disadvantages to free money, but you will usually have to satisfy strict and restrictive criteria. Government schemes to regenerate inner cities or repopulate rural districts sometimes have development funds attached to them that new businesses can draw on. Governments are normally keen to reduce unemployment and there are frequently schemes to help businesses which have strong recruitment plans.

Tips for raising finance

The decision on how to finance the start and growth of a business is one of the most important you will make. Be sure to discuss the options with your professional advisers, especially your accountant.

It pays to have the right kind of financial backing. Start by assessing your needs realistically.

1. Make full use your library. Many have excellent business centres and they will not charge you.

2. Try to find out how your competitors or similar businesses are financed. Draw up a chart. Look to see if patterns emerge in certain areas.
3. Get a list of business angels from your accountant. Start approaching them to see which might be interested in your type of business.
4. Find out what the best bank overdraft terms are likely to be.

What's in this chapter for you

Know what your plan is for
Understand what drives the professionals who will read it
Learn how to structure your plan
Develop a strategy for the meeting with your backers

> ❝ *Our business plan focused us incredibly. Getting our four different perspectives into one document needed real discipline.* ❞
> **– Jim Miller, Soldering Solutions**

Know what your plan is for

> ❝ *I thought we were writing our business plan for a private investor we had been introduced to. Three years on I realise that we were writing it for ourselves.* ❞
> **– Jim Miller**

By now you should have all the information you need to write a business plan. You have assessed your own skills and experience, your temperament and personal drives. You have thought about what type of business you are setting up and about the network of professional advisers that you will need – not just the obvious ones like accountants, solicitors and bank managers, but others like sales and marketing consultants, book-keepers, PR advisers, technology specialists and so on. You've considered the options for selling and marketing your product or service and you have thought about the financial records you will need to keep in order to maintain a firm grip on the business. You know how much money you need, not just to start the business but to run it smoothly, and you know the various methods of financing it. So who is the business plan for? The person or organisation you will approach for finance? Only partly.

Let's make sure you've covered all of the ground

You as a person	Do you fully understand your own personal objectives?	
	Are you as clear about your business objectives?	
	Are you physically up to it?	
	Is your family with you? (They have to live with you throughout this process!)	
You as a business-person	Do you fully understand the business you are planning – the market, the competition, the manufacturing or development processes?	
	Have you got enough experience?	
	Do you need to draft in extra skills at the outset?	
Market	Do you know how big it is? Where is it? How much it will cost you to get to it?	
	Does the competition look good? So how will you be better/different? Bad? You're kidding yourself!	
Product/Service	Do you know how much it will cost to make or develop it?	
	Do you know where you are going to do it?	
	Have you tested it? Does it work? Will customers want it even if it does?	
Price	Do you know the best price you can get?	
	How does that relate to your production costs? Do you get a reasonable gross margin?	

	Can you cope if you have to drop your prices?
Suppliers	Do you know who they are? Are they any good?
	Can they supply you at a price that gives you a margin?
	What credit terms will they give you?
Infrastructure	What premises will you need? Will they be enough?
	How much will that cost?
	Vehicles? Machinery? Computers?
People	Are you going to be an employer from the outset?
	How many staff? How much will you have to pay them?
	Are you aware of your legal responsibilities as an employer?
	Will they need training?
Financial controls	Have you prepared credible budgets and P&L and cashflow projections?
	If so, have you made assumptions. Are they valid?
	Have you prepared scenarios? What happens for instance if sales are half what you forecast? And what happens if they are double? Can you invest enough to keep pace?
Finance	How much do you need?
	What source would you prefer?
	Do you know how are you going to pay it back? When?

The business plan is also written for you. It's *your* blueprint for *your* future, not your bank's. It's a document that you have to believe in. If you don't, how can you expect anyone else to? There's just no point in trying to fiddle it.

Understand what drives the professionals who will read it

> **"** *Two days before our interview with our venture capitalist we had a practice run with our accountant. He pretended to be the semi-interested investor. It was incredibly helpful. Although we didn't have long to restructure our presentation we knew what the hot buttons and turn-offs in our plan would be.* **"**
> **– Adele Jones, Music promoter**

That said, other people are going to read your plan and they will use it, and their meetings with you, as a basis for a decision on whether or not to invest in your business. You want to influence them in the right direction so your plan has to be professionally prepared and presented. It's not enough for *just* you to believe in it, at least not if you are looking for financial backing of any description – even an overdraft facility.

> Try some internal role play. Become your accountant for half an hour. How would you react to this business proposal? Now your bank manager – he will be coming at it from a quite different perspective. Can you work it out? Now take a deep breath and be a venture capitalist for a while.

Let's take a bank manager as an example. When you go in to see him he will, broadly speaking, have five questions going through his mind (assuming, of course, that he likes your idea and thinks you're up to it):

- ○ *Do you need money from me?*
- ○ *If so, how much?*
- ○ *When?*
- ○ *How are you going to pay me back?*
- ○ *What security can you offer me against losing my money?*

It may sound like a hard and unsympathetic approach to the dream you have patiently been building layer by layer. But, let's face it, these are the real questions.

A private investor would come at it from a different angle. She would ask the same questions, but she would have a few more:

○ *How much equity will you give me?*
○ *Will I need to grant you share options to give you overall control of the business if it meets its targets?*
○ *How much 'sweat equity' can you put up?*
○ *What's my exit?*

By 'sweat equity' she means a sum of money that will be a lot to you if not to her (i.e. enough for the prospect of losing it to make you sweat). By 'exit' she means 'When can I realise my investment via flotation on a stock market, a trade sale or a management buy-out of my share of the business? Which of these is possible for this business I am looking at today?' She *has* to have a credible exit route.

The trick is to understand the motivation of the individual you are presenting to. Your plan needs to press different buttons for different types of investor.

Learn how to structure your plan

❝ *I thought it was going to be a real chore, but writing our business plan turned out to be a journey of discovery. I actually enjoyed it.*❞
– Adele Jones

The logical sequence in the checklist earlier in this chapter is one you can use for your business plan.

There are two main sections in a good plan – the commercial section and the financial section. The commercial section contains information about you, your product or service, the industry you operate in, market trends, production processes and so on. The financial section should contain your projected annual profit and loss forecast and monthly budget and cashflow forecasts. The more complicated your business is, the more likely you are to need to borrow. The larger your business is likely to be, the more important it is that these forecasts are very carefully drawn up. You will need to show how your business is going to develop and also show how you have arrived at your figures. You will also need to explain the assumptions that you have made.

The vital elements in a winning business plan

Introduction   This is like an executive summary of the whole plan. Give a brief overview of what the business is and how you see it developing. A punchy introduction to the market, production, overall package and so on, and a summary of the financial position should follow. You should probably write this section last as these one or two pages have to sell the whole plan. You want the person who is reading it to be excited enough by the general proposition to take the trouble to carry on!

Table of contents   You should include page numbers in this and list all the subheadings for each section as well.

Business details   You'll need to have a name for your business by now, a very important decision. What signals do you want to send to your customers and suppliers? What signal do you want to send to your competitors? If you are setting up a chain of rest homes don't call it something that suggests you're a trendy design agency.
   Also include in this section details of the type of business it will be (limited company, partnership, sole trader etc.).

Personal details   Give details of all those involved in managing the business. Its success will depend on their skills and experience, their dedication and motivation, so sell yourself and your colleagues. They represent a key factor in your eventual success.

Personnel details   Supply details of any staff you will be employing in the first two to three years. What will they be doing, what value will they be adding, how much will it cost you? If you are not putting people on your payroll give details of the freelance services you will be using.

Product/service   Describe it in detail but avoid technical specifications (unless it is a particularly complicated product for which you are looking for very substantial backing). What does it look and feel like? How big is it? If it's a service how will it be presented? If it's a product give information about further products that can be developed from it. How does it compare with your competitors' products or services? Also give details of your key suppliers, costs of supplies and credit terms.

Market/competition   If you have done your research thoroughly you should be able to give fairly accurate descriptions of your customers and their needs, of the size and geographical spread of the market, of the different segments within the market, and of competing products or services and where yours fits in. You need to do more than just list your competitors and their offerings. Try to give a clear description of *how* you will compete.

Sales/marketing   More detail on your competitive strategy – on pricing, sales, distribution, promotion and so on – all in the context of what your competition is doing. How much will it all cost?

Manufacturing (if appropriate)   What equipment and machinery will you need? Describe the manufacturing process and the attendant costs stage by stage.

Finance   All of the above needs to distilled into numbers. The minimum requirement will be your projected annual profit and loss and balance sheet forecasts and monthly budget and cashflow forecasts. If the business is complex you may need to supply break-even and sensitivity analyses, and wrestle with some financial ratios such as Return on Investment (ROI) and Return on Capital Employed (ROCE). Ask your accountant about the financial detail that will be expected of a business proposal on the particular scale you are planning.

Financing requirements   Here, depending on who you will be presenting the plan to, you will need to detail the amount of funds required and the timing. You will also need to think ahead to possible exit routes for equity partners.

❝ *I was talking a potential investor through our plan and I noticed a huge smudge at the bottom of the page he was looking at. I could tell that he was only giving me half his attention. I was sending one signal, but my plan was sending a different one.* ❞
–Sue Owen, Landscape gardener

A few words on presentation. You wouldn't turn up for a job interview in your gardening clothes would you? You would think about the image you want to present and dress appropriately. Your business plan does the same job for you. It should be well-written stylistically (to engage and maintain the reader's interest) and well-written technically (spelling mistakes and bad punctuation are a real turn-off). If your writing skills are limited it will pay you to get some copywriting help, or even a ghostwriter. Be honest with yourself – you don't have to be a brilliant writer but you need to have language skills. Have you? You also need to be numerate to run a business – do make sure that all your figures add up!

The plan also needs to be presented in a business-like, professional way, with clear headings and uncluttered pages. Use a high-quality white paper, but it doesn't have to be parchment. Put it in a simple spiral binding and make sure that the first page says what it is and who it is from.

Develop a strategy for the meeting with your backers

> **❝** *The first bank manager I met fazed me completely. I just hadn't thought enough about how to handle the meeting.* **❞**
> **– Wendy Hole**

You are meeting your bank manager next week. What are your objectives? What is it that you want to come out of the meeting with?

When you meet your potential backers to discuss your business plan you need to be absolutely clear in your own mind about your objectives. Of course you need to have detailed knowledge about your planned business, but that should be a given at this stage.

Write down the ideal outcomes of your meeting. What's the very best that you could get?

Once you know exactly what it is that *you* want you can develop a plan for getting it. Think about the position of the person you will be meeting. What will motivate her to back your ideas? What, in short, will ensure that your proposal is taken seriously?

Tips for putting together a winning business plan

A winning business plan can open up sources of finance and give your business the best possible chance of succeeding.

Your business plan should reflect your ambitions and drive but must be based firmly in reality.

1. Don't write it until you really believe it. Your own faith in your plan is an essential factor in your ability to present it persuasively.
2. The introduction is the key to grabbing the attention of your potential backers. Write it last. Your plan will develop even as you are composing it.
3. Make sure you have covered all the ground. Get it checked over by friends and family by all means but, most importantly, show it to your accountant before you unleash it on an unsuspecting world.
4. Never underestimate how much of a turn-off bad grammar and spelling mistakes can be. No matter how confident you are in your literary skills, ask someone who can spell to check your English!
5. Just as you have learnt to look at your product or service through the eyes of your customers, look at your plan through the eyes of an interested investor.